Pearls Out Of Pain

- a quest for God -

Rev Peter Hartley

Jesus Joy Publishing

Published and printed in Great Britain in 2014 by
Jesus Joy Publishing, a division of Eklegein Ltd.

© Peter Hartley, 2014

All rights reserved. The author gives permission for brief extracts from this book to be used in other publications provided that the following citation is stated.

Extract from *'Pearls Out Of Pain' by Peter Hartley, 2014 Jesus Joy Publishing used by permission'*.

All scripture quotations are taken from THE HOLY BIBLE, NEW INTERNATIONAL VERSION®, NIV® Copyright © 1973, 1978, 1984, 2011 by Biblica, Inc.™ Used by permission. All rights reserved worldwide.

Second Edition

First published by Diasozo Trust 1990

ISBN 978-1-90797-138-9

Jesus Joy Publishing

A division of Eklegein Ltd

www.jesusjoypublishing.co.uk
20140601

Dedication

I lovingly dedicate this book
To my dear wife
Hilary
The Companion of my Quest
and the
Partner of my Pilgrimage

A Word of Personal Testimony

"Young man, you have a tumour at the base of the skull."

The were the very words of that leading and kind Leading Consultant at Rochester Infirmary to me in 1972, after my appointment at their X-ray Department.

I was 32 years of age and the tumour in my head had been growing for a number of years. It had destroyed the pituitary gland and the fossa in which the pituitary lay had been eroded to paper thickness. A chromophobe adenoma they called it. My hormone imbalances and prolactin levels were sky-high and thyroid was nil.

The presence and growth of the tumour certainly explained the struggle of those years, desperately trying to keep up and to cope. The optic nerves began to waver under the strain and pressure of the tumour. The pain was bad, but the emotional and nervous trauma was far worse. After many years of looking forward, my hopes of overseas service for the Kingdom of God had to go.

Six months before the diagnosis, Hilary and I stood at the altar to say, *"In sickness and in health... till death us do part"*. Much prayer had been offered, for me, throughout this country. Indeed, from all over the world has come the promise and support of prayer.

Something of a casualty, I was ordered to rest. The Lord made provision for me to spend a week at a Home of Healing, in East Sussex. I drove there, hard, bleak and desperately in need. Here, Hilary could not come. I must go alone. Rarely has she left my side and never have I been separated from her care and love.

The Home's first effect upon me was to lead me to my room to weep. Here was love and healing in a practical way. I had not known this before. Thursday was a Service of Holy Communion and the 'Laying on of hands'. That morning, about 9 a.m., I became wonderfully aware of the Lord's presence, in a measure unknown before. I feared His presence might go away, but it did not! I also felt a powerful heart-warming sense of faith. Thus it was that I made my way to the Chapel for the 10 a.m. Service. I spent several moments on my knees just gazing at the Cross and a memorial of the Lord.

I saw the Lord coming towards me! He was so real! His arms were stretched out to me! The Lord was present to heal others too, but it was as though He was there for me, just me!

Was this an end to what had seemed a silent heaven for so long? Oh my dear Lord Jesus; He was coming to me! He came and stood by my side. How often I have prayed for others, "That they might have the Lord's presence right by their side". Here He was, right by MY side! It was wonderful! How can I describe the heavenly reality of those moments? As I stood in His embrace, He said, *"I love You."* There were no words which I needed to hear more than these. Now I heard Him for myself, not someone else telling me! He told me Himself! This was music sweeter than anything I have ever heard. I responded to Him and this was what I said, "Lord, I love You too! It was a conversation almost too precious to utter, but I tell it for His glory alone.

I then saw myself kneeling, and later I knelt at the same place as in my vision. I saw the Lord was just behind me. As I knelt I saw, as it were, a cloak or shawl rising from my back and shoulders. I knew in those moments, that shawl was the sum total of all that hindered my wholeness in Christ. It was my disease and all its consequences, and by all, I mean all. All in me that was contrary to the nature, grace and love of the Lord. As I looked, I saw the Lord stretch out His hand. He took the cloak and, with one omnipotent action of His arm, He cast it away. The pit was dark and its billows curled in blackness. I saw that cloak or shawl no more. I was healed! The Lord who had been pleased to heal others through my hands, now healed me.

I remember and clearly saw what happened next. I asked the Lord, 'what about those drugs, tablets and pills that I take every day of my life?' They were in my room, all eight or so containers of them. I had them in a Boot's plastic bag. It was as though the Lord picked up this plastic bag, as one would pick up a smelly oil rag with the tips of one's fingers. This He also threw away with the same action of His omnipotent arm! He threw them to the same place as the cloak that had gone from my back and shoulders! By no means did I understand this to be an action of scorn. Those drugs etc. had kept me alive! This was an action of His loving power that would give new life to me.

But all was not over. I saw now a throne. It was before me - in front of me! It was where my Lord reigned! It was His throne. What a sight it was!

Introduction

I believe that the Lord requires honesty from us, thus what you read here must glorify the Lord. The crisis which required surgery on my head was 40 years ago. While I was at College in Cambridge, the tumour returned and I was advised to have a course of Radiotherapy.

The Lord did not heal my pituitary tumour, and I have had to live with its consequences, having to retire from the ministry in my mid fifties.

I still believe that God is able to heal though He has chosen to call me to a different path, perhaps to share with him, *"In the fellowship of His sufferings"*. I trust that what is here will glorify the Lord, and be of help to you as you seek to find *"His strength made perfect in your weakness."*

God bless you and fill your days and nights with his Love and with His Divine and Holy Presence, and perfect peace.

I trust that you will find what is in this book, **'Pearls Out Of Pain'** both helpful and a blessing to you. If you wish to write to me I shall be thrilled to hear from you.

Peter Hartley
Polegate
East Sussex
BN22 5BG

Contents

Quest of My Life
- 19   Quest of My life
- 23   The Best of My Life
- 24   The Love of My Life
- 25   Ashes, Agony or Aspiration
- 28   Changing and Abiding
- 29   Sunrise - the Break of Day
- 30   Make Yourself at Home Lord
- 32   A Close Walk
- 32   A Safe Hiding Place
- 33   An Aspiring Christian
- 34   Lord of My Everything
- 35   Lord, I'm Coming Home
- 35   Climb Every Mountain
- 36   Making the Most of My Moments
- 37   Come Follow Me
- 37   Koinonia - Fellowship: Me and the Lord
- 40   Let Us Go Over

Inspired of Scripture
- 43   The Love Slave
- 44   About the 23rd Psalm
- 46   About Psalm 33:1-6
- 47   Psalm 121 : A Paraphrase
- 48   Four Philippian 'Alls'
- 50   Marah - Bitterness
- 51   Let Not Your Heart be Troubled
- 52   Let This Mind be in You
- 53   His Strength Made Perfect
- 54   Pressing Towards the Mark

About Prayer
- 59   Lord Teach Us How To Pray
- 65   A Birthday Prayer
- 66   A True Heart Cry
- 67   What are You Trying to Say, Lord?
- 68   I Can't But You Can
- 69   Morning Prayer
- 70   Waiting To Worship

71   A Praying Christian
71   What are You Saying, Lord?
72   By Prayer and Supplication
72   Prayer Leaps the Barrier of Miles
73   Oh, To Touch You
74   My Morning Dew
75   Oh My Father
76   The Early Morning Dew
76   Open! On the Godward Side

Seasons
81   Birthdays are Milestones
81   New Year Aspirations
82   Memories of Mother
83   Abiding Security
84   Infant Wonderful
84   Monarch of the Manger
85   Oh Bethlehem
85   The Day Star
87   God's Passover Lamb
89   Preciousness Poured Out
90   The Lord Turned and Looked
90   About the Suffering of Jesus
92   My Child, Behold My Hands
93   A Living Lord Jesus

Ponderings & Musings
101   A More Excellent Way
103   An Open Heart
104   For the Conversion of St Paul
104   Grace Did Much More Abound
105   The Lane of Life
106   The Secret of the Shadows
107   For a Daughter and Her Mum
108   The Eye that Guides
108   Simplicity
108   Sea - The Soul Mender
109   Cords and the Cross
110   The Harbour
111   A Royal Rest
111   A Beautiful Life
112   About Signposts

114	Helping and Caring
114	God is Love
116	About the Lord
117	A Home Christ Loved
118	Light of the World
119	Sir, the Well is Deep
120	To Look and Look at Him
121	The Master's Men
123	A Sharing Christian
123	Lord Jesus, What are You Doing?
125	Everything in His Hands
127	A Caring Christian
127	Sufficient Grace
128	Fear Not
128	Just Until the Day Break
128	Learning To Lean
129	Oh! Those Shoulders
129	Sovereign Storms Over
130	The Cross - His and Mine
130	A Time to be Glad
130	In Appreciation
131	My Note to You Today
131	Thank You
132	Just Being Honest, Lord
133	The Encourager's Pen
133	Amazing Love
135	When I Can't Understand
137	Alphabetical List of Poems

Quest of My Life

Quest of My life

Somehow, when lost in the maze of my years,
With no inner presence to comfort my fears;
How often my eyes were a fountain of tears,
Life seemed like a valley where the mist never clears.

My soul often asked in the black hours of night,
If only I had but a glimpse of the light;
But grope as I might for the dawn of delight,
My call but re-echoed, reflected my plight.

How poignant the moments adrift and alone,
How painful the music, how dreadful the drone;
How passion was moment'ry and mocked me to moan,
How futile and meaningless, a soul on its own.

I tasted, but hungry of heart I remained,
I touched, then my soul was but sullied and stained;
I tried, but my mind became moulded and maimed,
I tumbled in poverty's pain, powerless and chained.

"Is there no one to help me?" I cried in despair,
In sheer desperation, it must have been prayer;
My soul in an agony, fists beating the air!
Is there no one to hear me beyond the 'out there'?

It seemed e'er my lips had but uttered this cry,
A consciousness gripped me that help was close by;
My eyes drifted upward, yes, up to the sky,
Where the light of a star caught the sight of my eye.

I felt in that moment my hopelessness die,
The floods of my tears were beginning to dry,
A massive compelling, a presence close by,
Which urged me to follow that star in the sky.

The sky was still dark but ne'er hid from my view,
Through a break in the clouds came that light shining through;
I clung to a hope, a hope that was new,
That the light far above me, had purpose, was true.

It suddenly dawned on me as day after day,
When, but for my star I would sure lose my way;
But a pilgrim I was and a pilgrim I'll stay,
The quest of my life to pursue, come what may.

My mind then recaptured those days way back there,
A beautiful mother, her soft silken hair;
The touch of her hands was the touch of her care,
But memory of mother was a memory of prayer.

My way long and dreary, how dreadful the thought,
I feared it too late to see what I sought;
A burden which clung to me was all I had brought,
Was it to be in vain? Was all for nought?

But then, just to pause and to look up and see,
The light that was sent seemed so special to me;
My pace would be quickened for I longed to be free,
I left where I came from, where I go it must be.

Far away, yet before me but piercing the night,
I saw what I can but say was a wonderful sight;
In shafts of great splendour both golden and light,

Oh, that beautiful hillside so gloriously bright!
Towards it I sped, for now how could I tire?
And then, in a moment, the clouds seemed on fire;
Now rank upon rank of heaven's own great massed choir,
The song which they sang rose but higher and higher.

But after a while having gone a fair pace,
The beautiful light stayed a pathway to trace;
In a moment it seemed I had come to the place,
For a while, I could rest, oh blest breathing space.

In utter amazement I stood at the door,
With words just above, "For the rich and the poor";
Poor though I was, I felt I could be sure,
Of a welcome, love's kindness, so holy so pure.

I stood by that door awhile just trying to know;
Once and again my hand to the door latch would go:
Though a strong hand restrained me and a dark voice said "No";
I was caught in love's torrent - irresistible flow.

No longer persuaded by self-passion to try;
No longer perplexed by doubt's ponderous why;
No longer possessed by despair's passionate cry;
No longer pervaded by Sin's perilous sigh.

To my humbled astonishment, how could it be?
That the door once before me is now opening I see,
Then I knew that the door had been opened for me,
And all I need do was to enter and see.

The lintel was lowly, but the entrance was wide,
My shoulders were bent but my feet were inside;
Then casting a glance as to where I could hide,
I buried my face in my hands, for a while, and I cried.

I felt for a moment my heart it must break,
But my tears were not those of despair's tragic make;
In so humble a place there began to awake,
A calm understanding that it was for my sake.

Not a soul saw me enter the stable that night,
The ground was so holy, my footsteps were light;
But before my own eyes was the wonderful sight,
Of a Baby! Oh, a Baby! Oh, dawn of delight.

It seemed for a moment the world's concourse met there,
With a beautiful mother, how divine was her care;
And then as though angels encircled the air,
I was alone with the Babe and my prayer.

I knelt at the manger to gaze at His face,
His eyes meeting mine with their shame and disgrace;
Could it be that this Child Who was so full of grace,
Would provide for my soul a safe hiding place?

As I rose from my knees and stepped from His side,
No longer forsaken, I knew love would abide;
No longer forlorn, I could always confide,
For ever a refuge, a place, where, I could hide.

But what did I see not long before day?
The Child's lovely mother the lamp took away;
A mystery descended O'er the place where He lay,
So meek and so mild, fast asleep on the hay.

The lamp was hung high in that stable so bare,
A shadow cast O'er the Babe lying there;
It seemed to my heart as I rose up to stare,
The shadow was that of a Cross, oh infant, so fair.

I knew as I left as the first light of day,
That a pilgrim I was and a pilgrim I'd stay;
An inward voice told me as I went on my way,
That the Cross I had seen before breaking of day -

Would be raised once again on a hill far away,
And the sins I had carried would be nailed there to stay;
But the manger I'd left, held the price that must pay,
But a pilgrim I was and a pilgrim I'll stay.

The Best of My Life

Lord, not just the ashes of year after year,
Or merely my hopes intermingled with fear;
Not only the failures stained by many a tear,
Yet withholding from You all the things I hold dear.

How often in childhood, those innocent days,
Skillfully handled, the little life prays;
While watching intensely its wide eyes will gaze,
Then quaintly in song, sing a paean of praise.

Yet childhood soon passes, and youth becomes man,
The life will set foot on life's ponderous span;
Its choice it must make; for no other can,
The feet that will run, are the feet that once ran.

That life is mine and the choice I must make,
Which way will I go? What road shall I take?
Breezes that blow, may be gales that will shake;
Waves that lapped gently, could be billows that break!

Just as I am, I come, at Your altar to stand,
As I give You my heart, will You give me Your hand?
While I cling to Your cross, could Your grace, too, expand?
To embrace a poor sinner who cannot understand.

Why You hung on a cross, with Your arms opened wide?
While You purchased a way in my heart to abide;
By Your grace, Oh my Saviour, my Lord crucified,
The best of my life is with You at my side.

The Love of My Life

Oh, let me love You, Lord, today,
    Just You alone;
Pray, may no other rival take,
    What is Your own.

Then let my love be first for You,
    No second place;
Meaner attractions may they not,
    Conceal Your face!

While loving others let me learn,
    Your love's control;
Love me, lest any other love,
    O'ertake my soul.

Lord of my heart, a heart so prone,
    This human thing;
And yet so safe while sheltering,
    Beneath Your wing.

Lord of my love, Lord of my life,
    Oh let me rest;
I seek no other pillow than,
    Upon Your breast.

Ashes, Agony or Aspiration

The agony of ashes, Lord,
To an aspiring soul;
When health by havoc heaves apart,
And longs to be made whole!
Where e'en the call of God does shake,
'Neath the kind Shepherd's rod;
Across love's lifeline lies a lane:
Made by the feet of God!

Tested is truth - truth's trust on trial,
That error be defined;
The homeless heart though hurt must have:
Its happiness refined.
Ah! Hapless haze, horizon's view,

The sight of you impaired;
Last footstep's next but one not seen:
Its mark lies undeclared.

Included not, kind cry of Christ,
Your grasp of Me this hour;
Nor tremble tried and tested child:
But see My keeping power.
Forgive the finity of faith,
Fettered to flesh and blood;
For heaviness it fails to fly:
Into the arms of God !

The night of need lies not beyond,
Our living, loving, Lord;
Victorious faith's vicariousness:
Release the powerful word.
Then let the mighty mountain move,
Let miracle leap forth;
Ah! faithless soul here mercy's grace:
A gracious Saviour's worth !

Then shall a well of water spring,
Within the wilderness;
Forth from the rock thy honey bring:
To heal and then to bless.
Thy soul in God shall then rejoice,
Glory to Him belong;
May God through grace in thee observe:
Maturer faith more strong.

Those times, my Lord, I would not choose,
To pass that way again;
Yet in Your will mine I must lose:
Such loss is surely gain.
And yet, Oh Christ, this would I ask,
I plead, may it live on;
Your living, loving, promised word:
Made mine through Your dear Son.

My child, there lies ahead of you,
A wide, wide open door;
The Father placed it there for you:
'Tis open evermore.
What God has opened, none can shut,
Dear child, just grasp this fact;
No throne but Mine could make it such:
Omnipotent an act !

Ah yes, my Lord, what were those words,
Like silver in the sand;
You promised me Yourself, Oh God:
From then, You took my hand.
My presence it shall go with thee,
And I will give thee rest;
Lord grant that I might ever know:
Your peace within my breast .

Changing and Abiding

Things always change, the old makes way,
Makes way for new, 'things' have their day;
The wise world's view and thus they say:
Discarded things are thrown away.
Familiar scenes take on new stance,
We view our history's distance;
With gratitude we cast our glance:
As progress comes with swift advance.

'Adieu for aye', into the past,
Inferior's unlikely last;
Its temporary vantage cast:
Outmode, forgetfully, so fast.
The wise for this, no mourning wake,
As life's realities will shake;
Redundant obsolescence take:
Superiority's best make.

Things differ, no equality,
The wise observe validity;
They cling to true priority:
For time attests true quality.
But then I turn to things divine,
Experience has made truth mine;
The well defined -it can but shine:
Pure gold, the fire did well refine.

Foundation's faith remains the same,
The cross still stands - through flood and flame;
There still exists no other name:
God's love, unrivalled sacred fame.
I would the older paths discern,
From apostolic lips would learn;
The old, old story, let it burn:
Oh God, from You, I cannot turn.

Sunrise - the Break of Day

The sun at break of day does bring,
Across the sea its sparkling thrill;
But just to look, my soul takes wing,
As loveliness spreads O'er the hill.

The clouds are golden with delight,
Ah, distant scene, so clear today;
The main roars back with all its might,
The sky, so wonderful, but pray -

Who gave the sun its healing wing?
But, Oh! the sun of righteousness;
Around heart-wounds e'en grief must sing,
While standing there in human dress.

Perfection plucks the cords that play,
And terror melts in tenderness;
Oh, sight sublime, so let me stay;
And not forget such splendidness.

The rocks which call to me today,
Which keep me here their clasp so strong;
While ocean waves must dash and spray;
How great to know that I belong -

The rock is here and here to stay,
Winged creatures swoop, and stay, what song!
My soul do not forget the day;
When many multitudes -the throng -

They too, once stood upon the rock,
Their arms embraced the rising sun;
Then given a place among faith's flock;
The fight of faith was then begun.

It seems time's tide, yet often more,
So sorrow's swell, so soon a flood,
But shining there, along the shore,
The sun, and oh! My Lord, my God!

Make Yourself at Home Lord

When one day I led the Saviour.
To the throne room of my life:
It was there He stood confronted,
By my need and by my strife!
In my night and in my sorrow,
In my shame and in my plight;
Then He took me as He found me,
Turned my darkness into light!

Were it not for 'grace abounding',
And the word 'forgiven' there;
How could I bring my dear Saviour,
To this temple of despair?
Ah, but what transforming power!
Changed that scene of wrong within!
By His love and in His mercy,
Did that gracious work begin!

Sometimes peaceful, sometimes painful,
In that citadel of mine;
As the radiant Lord of glory,
Into each recess did shine.
Thus exposing what could never,
Share the place where Christ must reign;
Oh, my Master, purge the dwelling,
Spare my soul but not the pain.

Nought for self but all for Jesus,
This the prayer I offer, Lord;
All my heart Your shrine for ever,
Loving Saviour, living Word.
Having conquered, Lord, I'm longing,
That You will Your cords extend;
Take me deeper, lift me higher,
'Til my pilgrim days shall end.

A Close Walk

Ah, Lord, there lies before me,
A choice, I must decide;
How close I walk with Jesus,
The Lamb of God, Who died!
Christ, just a brief acquaintance,
Or, always side by side;
Or follow at a distance,
From Him the crucified!
Please, could it be, Lord Jesus,
Oh, will You make it plain;
Just what it means to know You,
Pray, tell me once again.

A Safe Hiding Place

In grace there is a place I see,
Where hearts are citadels for Thee;
Though trouble ne'er may bypass me,
Beyond its reach the heart may be.
I see there is a hiding place,
Where I can find preserving grace;
What arms, dear Lord, where love's embrace,
Inspires my song and sees Your face.

An Aspiring Christian

Have I stopped climbing, Lord?
Has my soul ceased to aspire?
Does my spirit no longer surge forward?
Is my heart no longer on fire?
Have I lost the vision You gave me?
Does the summit no longer appeal?
Must it be that no more I may look up and see,
With the pull of the peaks but a memory, real?

Can I start climbing again, Lord?
Will You match Your pace to suit mine?
Can it be that Your footsteps be plain, Lord?
Will You give me Your presence divine?
May the form of the dear Son of God,
Go before till the journey shall end;
Thus while tracing the way of my Lord,
I shall never lose sight of my Friend!

And yet as I climb with a heart that must rise,
With eyes for my Christ on the mountainside;
I feel I have learned with tear-brimmed eyes,
Some lessons of life in the school of my Guide.
The secrets, that only the valley can share,
For life's priceless values are only worthwhile;
To such as go forth to love and to care,
And emerge from the valley of sorrow and smile.

Climbing with You, Lord, teach me to pray,
Unveiling the heights and depths of Your word;
For power, for peace, for Your presence each day,
With the incomparable love of an infinite Lord!

Take my fears, give me faith, take conceited ambition,
Grant me oceans of grace, patient heart of my Guide;
For Your glory I climb to the summit of vision,
Not forgetting there is room for a world in Your side.

Lord of My Everything

    Lord of all grace, dear grace that called,
        Called us though we had passed You by:
    What grace was this when at our side,
        Showed us the Cross on which You died.

    Lord of all peace, then let me come,
        To the safe refuge of my Guide;
    Lest I should seek another place,
        Outside the refuge of Your grace.
    Lord of my life, I bring to Thee,
        This life that has no room for me;
    Can I withhold my all from Thee,
        When You gave all for love of me?

    Lord of my weakness and each fear,
        Lord of my grief; Lord of each tear;
    Lord of each conflict - right and wrong,
        Lord of each triumph and each song!

    Lord of all glory - all is Thine;
        I may not touch what is not mine:
    Mine is to make the Saviour known,
        Mine is to cry, "Behold the Lamb."

Lord, I'm Coming Home

Lord, I think that I am learning,
    As through this poor world I roam;
I'm a pilgrim and a stranger:
    By Your grace I'm coming home.
There is nought on earth to keep me,
    There are no attractions here;
I am coming home to heaven,
    By Your grace I'll see You there.

Climb Every Mountain

Lord Jesus, there are mountains,
That confront my life today;
Some seem so impossible,
And they will not go away!
Did You, Lord, not say to me,
Though thy faith be e'er so small;
If you will but trust in Me,
Then you can remove them all!
Some mountains are for climbing,
With their steep and rugged face;
Yet do not be discouraged,
When but slowly is thy pace.
For speed is not essential,
In the race that lies ahead;
I'll always go before you,
In My footprints you may tread!
My child, I loved the mountains,

It was there I went to pray;
There it was I prayed for you,
Long before the break of day.
You will find grace for climbing,
And my help will always be;
On hand for all My children,
Who will simply trust in Me!

Making the Most of My Moments

How swiftly the moments are passing;
    History written - each tale is told:
The tale, are some pages still missing,
    From pages all edged with pure gold?

For some folk these pages are tarnished,
    Their deeds full of cruelty and shame!
Life's story, their object is anguish;
    No love because hate is their name!

For others, life means simply caring;
    To cheer and to love and to share:
Life's joy is in helping and bearing;
    The moment of need finds them there.

Life's mountains, Oh God, are for climbing,
    May I help my brother climb too?
The summit is only appealing,
    As I stand there my brother with you!

Come Follow Me

Lord, as along the lanes of life,
    I walked, I felt I walked with You.
Yet weak and so inadequate,
    There seemed but one thing I must do;
I must respond to Him Whose call,
    Whose eyes with urgent passion bright:
Enabling call, "Come follow Me,
    Easy My yoke, My burden light !"

My hand within the clasp of His;
    Inside the circle of His grace:
Though oft O'erwhelmed - unworthiness;
    He found this servant child a place.
The glorious gospel, blessed God;
    Entrusted, thus committed, Lord:
Oh God, I pray for faithfulness;
    Anchored to Your eternal word.

Koinonia - Fellowship: Me and the Lord

Do I discern the purpose, Lord, of Calvary?
    One that my separated soul, at peace may be:
What word is this, engraved by grace, "Forgiven child";
    As sure as once, trust there was none, by sin beguiled.
A gracious gift was given to me, the gift of sight;
    My quickened soul at liberty, walked in the light.

I found I loved that sacred place, called Calvary:
    Oh Lamb of God, You love the world, yet You love me!
The Pilot of a million lives -Your hand holds mine!
    I've found a Friend to walk with me, He is divine.
The way, not wide, but Oh my Guide, He walked with me;
    We journeyed on, and Oh the joy, He talked to me!
But what was this, a sacred bond, which was so strong;
    There is a family to which, I now belong:
My Friend, a secret shared with me, in fellowship,
    But I must e'er resemble Him by life and lip.
A promise which I treasure most, given by my Guide,
    That He would never go away or leave my side !
Ah, fellowship's fine faithfulness, that loveth me,
    For all our fellowship is found at Calvary;
The more I gaze upon His wounds, and hear His cry:
    The more the cost confronts my care for Christ to die.
Can I withhold, dear Lord from Thee, when You gave all?
    Then grant me grace, Lord, to respond unto Your call.
Lord, take my hand in fellowship, to spread Your word,
    And then wherever You may send, make Your voice heard:,
Yet in that hour, please may I be, thus satisfied;
    To know that You are standing there, right by my side:
Please may my trust be simple, Lord, may love be such;

To know that You're within the reach, that faith can touch.

To touch You when my heart, would fail and fearful be;
    Then touch You in life's darkest hours, too dark to see:
To touch You when it seems, so hard to understand;
    And touch You when a friend so dear, withdraws the hand.
When clouds are low and mists would rise, to touch You there,
    Then standing in the sunshine, God has answered prayer !

Within the bond of fellowship, we make our way,
    To that place of cloudless light, when break of day,
Has scattered every shadow; every storm is still;
    Where everything is subject, to the Father's will:
For now, my child I give you, "all sufficient grace";
    Just live where you may always, clearly see My face.

Let Us Go Over

My friend, a tempest fills your sky,
    The breakers roll, the wind - a gale;
Your faith is tried, your heart asks why?
    But this I share, Christ will not fail !
Just to know the Lord is Master,
    On board the vessel of your life;
Just to prove His love is vaster,
    Than any ocean's threatening strife.
When the Lord said, "Let's go over,
    To life's far off distant shore",
Then no power will take you under;
    To be lost for evermore.
When it seems the Lord is sleeping,
    And you feel He does not care;
In the shadows He is standing;
    And, yes, the Lord will answer prayer.
Then will come that powerful moment,
    When Christ the King will speak the word;
He will still the raging torrent,
    And when the gale His voice has heard,
By your side will be your shelter;
    What a Saviour, what a Friend:
Here is love no power can alter,
    And a peace that knows no end!

Inspired of Scripture

The Love Slave

Exodus 21:2-6

My servant, come here, for in this the sixth year,
To one of your station, emancipation!
My God has commanded and the law has demanded,
Your liberty gained and your freedom proclaimed,
There is nothing can hold you, and lo, I have told you,
The door is now open and I give you your freedom,
To go and not stay on this wonderful day.

But alone you must go, for the day of your woe,
Found you poverty-stricken with no one to quicken,
The throb of your heart and so you must part,
With all you have gained while your service remained,
To a master who sought the slave that he bought,
My servant, go free, you no longer need be,
A servant to me, you are free!

My master, I plead, in the hour of my need,
I have dreaded the day you might send me away,
May no way be found how I might be bound ,
For service, for ever, separate never,
From all I hold dear and those who are near,
Must it be that I part? Entwined is the heart,
By a love, that though oceans break, and dash my emotions.

Love's bond is the hand, thus humbly I stand,
To beg of my master, pray let not disaster,
Be the price of my freedom and the cost of a lonesome,
Walk with but memories store and a life that is poor,

Existence bereft for nothing is left,
To a servant now free who no longer need be,
Of service to thee, must I be free?

My servant, a plan, is designed for the man,
In whose life love's compelling, Redeemer indwelling,
With his heart he must say "I cannot go away".
In complete consecration, I have chosen my station,
For the master who bought me all true values has taught me,
With a more excellent way in His service I'll stay,
But the love of a servant must give place to the fervent.

Love giving, love taking, of those who are making,
A partnership, blending, that never has ending,
And the fruit of our love are but signs of above,
Where the love of a Father, in Whose service I'd rather-
Though my freedom is mine, what love, so divine;
Let the mark of your grace now be made on my face,
"Free to go", You have told me, but compelled I shall serve Thee.

About the 23rd Psalm

Oh, Shepherd Friend; for ever may it be,
Until the end, please, I would follow Thee:
No other voice to take the place of Thine;
No other choice than that which made Thee mine.

May I not want, what never Your sweet will,
Allows for me - You do not choose that ill,
Shall satisfy, or rest content until;
My longing soul, Yourself, my vessel fill.

Ah, tempter's power, vain gild and glint increase!
True love grows cold, heart rest in God does cease!
Oh, blessed constraint, Good Shepherd, ne'er release;
In Your dear hands, here only I find peace!

When all Your waves and billows, though no harm,
Are gone O'er me, and Jordan crossed, this Psalm;
He led me here, so strong my Shepherd's arm:
Lord, lead me there, by waters still and calm.

Just as I am, I come, Oh make me whole;
A pilgrim child - a world - help me to roll,
On one so strong, all that the world takes toll
Oh, Shepherd kind, I pray restore my soul.

Good Shepherd, where You lead, there I must go;
Where e'er it be, how wonderful to know,
That with each step, Your love shall surely show:
Lord Jesus Christ, the name whose praise must flow.

Kind Shepherd, when the call shall come to me,
And I come home, across death's narrow sea;
No shadowed vale; no wave shall evil be,
For I shall have Your own dear company.

Dear Lord, in death, no evil need I fear;
You are with me, that which I hold most dear,
Than unchastised, I would Your rod appear:
Uncomforted, I would Your staff be near.

Good Lord, I stand on what Your promise says;
For all my need; the story of my days:
My table spread, the proof that all Your ways,
Are pleasantness, thus may my life be praise.

Bewildered, Lord, some fail to comprehend;
Because of You, some bitterly contend:
Anointing One, on me Your Spirit send;
My life O'erflow, until my journey's end.

My Shepherd Friend, my prayers would now ascend;
For goodness, Lord, I ask that You will lend,
To me, for life, while mercy's arms extend:
Oh, gracious Lord, love's giving knows no end.

I come to You, and at Your altar stand,
Lord, take my heart, Good Shepherd take my hand;
No other way, than what Your will has planned:
Your house, for life, I wait on Your command!

About Psalm 33:1-6

Dear Lord, I would be glad in Thee;
Covered by Him, whose righteousness,
Shines best, when all the world can see,
The Lord I love, the name I bless.

Let instruments tell forth His praise;
Ne'er can it be too great the choir:
With harmony, love Him, Whose ways,
Awake in you love's grand desire.

Oh, Lord of Lords, the song is new;
Where love is true, love's heart will yearn:
For praise, all barriers can break through,
Blessed are they who love, who learn.

Worthy the One Whose word is right,
Let truth respond with cheerful voice;
His word, His works, proclaim His might;
Then raise your song and sing! Rejoice!

Loud be the praise, rejoice with mirth,
To Him Whose ways are just and right;
The Lord is good to all the earth,
Then let the earth in Him delight.

Whose powerful word made heaven to be,
His breath brought forth heaven's glorious host!
Yet that same word still cares for thee,
For man to God must matter most.

Psalm 121 : A Paraphrase

To the hills of my God I will lift up my eyes,
The hills of the Lord which point up to the skies;
My help cometh surely, He has given His word:
So these are my hills and the Lord is my Lord.

He made every mountain, and each rivulet;
He made every rainbow. He made the sunset:
Then is He not able, His help to afford,
To those who look up to, the hill of the Lord?

Oh hills, Oh my helper, I must travel on,
My pilgrimage calls me, the day is soon done -
The perils, the dangers, my wandering feet,
You promised to keep me in safety complete.

Your love will not weary. Your eye never tires;
Your grace is abounding; it never expires:
My Keeper is with me; my feet will not roam;
For His hills are my hills and I'm going home.

The sun will not hurt you and fear not the night,
The Lord is your shade on the left and the right;
No danger need daunt you; no foe can prevail:
My arms are around you and they cannot fail.

My hills, Oh my shelter, my guardian divine;
The sovereign protector of this life of mine:
O'er life's ebb and flow now the waves cannot foam;
I'm safe on that hillside for I have come home.

Four Philippian 'Alls'

"Rejoice in the Lord always: and again I say, Rejoice."
Philippians 4:4

For this, my heart would ask of Thee,
My gracious Lord, Your joy might be;
Bestowed on me for all to see:
Yet for Your name so gloriously.
No glory does it bring to you,
When sadness does my life pursue;
So strange, my Lord, and yet so true:

That praise will make a way right through.
Let me rejoice through all my days,
And bring my sacrifice of praise.

"The peace of God that passes all understanding."
Philippians 4:7

My Lord, I may not understand,
Within the hollow of Your hand;
A place of peace divinely planned.
What of the travails of the way?
What of the fight of faith each day?
What of His side where I must stay?
Your peace, my mind it cannot grasp,
Yet that same peace my heart would clasp;
Oh, Prince of Peace, 'twas Your bequest:
A peace that keeps the heart at rest.

"I can do all things through Christ Who strengthens me."
Philippians 4:13

So weak the frailty of our frame,
Might, not possessed by human name;
How sacred is His holy flame:
Oh Christ, Your power remains the same,
Not to be powerful would I ask;
When love confronts me with a task:
Yet in my weakness let me choose,
My weakness in Your power to lose;
That through this life You may diffuse:
Your power, and then Your servant use.

"My God shall supply all your need according to His riches in glory by Christ Jesus."

Philippians 4:19

I do not know your needs, my friend,
I am not by your side to lend;
A helping hand, but I can send:
Encouragement, for God has seen,
Philippians four and verse nineteen;
Points to the infinite supply:
And through the Christ Who reigns on high,
Are riches God will not deny;
To those who on His word rely:
And trust in Him Whose help is nigh.

Marah - Bitterness

Exodus 15:22-27

In memory there was a day, I found a thing,
The wilderness; my weary way, fury did fling;
So circumstance my soul did spray, and Oh, its sting:
Perceiving, powerless to pray - a bitter spring.

Engraved the history of those years, I came in haste,
And stooped, and did in spite of fears, those waters taste;
False physician disguised appears, my wounds to paste:
Then questioning through floods of tears, Oh why this waste?

But mercy soon was at my side, I saw a Tree,
It seemed that love with massive stride, caught up with me;
A hand, that Cross, I turned to hide - a tragedy!
Reflected in that bitter tide, a Cross, I see.

'Marah' no longer, love revealed, those waters, sweet,
The Cross, my bitter waters healed, my needs to meet;
That very Cross, grace found me there, its work complete:
For there the covenant was signed, at Jesus' feet.

Let Not Your Heart be Troubled

Let not your heart be in distress;
Your trust in God and Christ confess:
There is a home you will possess;
Be certain of My faithfulness.

I shall prepare with carefulness;
A home of perfect blessedness:
When I, shall with immortal dress;
Rise to My Royal Kingliness!

Remember that My prayerfulness;
Is touched by loving tenderness:
I knew the path of loneliness;
The human road of weariness.

And yet, no moment of distress;
Lies buried in forgetfulness:
Bequeathed in My trustworthiness;
A promise for your hopefulness.

I will come again with powerfulness;
For you will share My gloriousness:
But now, will you My love express;
And wait with patient watchfulness?

Let This Mind be in You

The Lord is seated on His throne so high,
We see Him there, but first we see Him die!
Golgotha first and then His exaltation;
That we might know how great is our salvation!

Oh, Holy Spirit, take the mind of Him,
Then take ours, too, and make them pure within;
It is Your work, sweet Spirit, it is Thine,
To take of Christ and make it freely mine!

A humble mind is what I seek to know,
That He may find the weakness that will show;
His power made perfect through the human frame,
With all the glory given to His name!

His person so divine, what mystery,
That He is Lord - the Christian's ecstasy!
Though God, He did not grasp equality,
But with what love accepted our humanity.

Co-regent, He rejected reputation,
Accepting in its place a servant's station;
It mattered not how low in estimation,
Deliberately He chose humiliation.

No test, but what He was subjected,
No trial for expediency rejected;
Anguish, He never underestimated,
And even death upon the cross, He tasted!

His throne unequalled now in earth and heaven,
A high transcendent name He has been given;
Where every knee bows in humiliation,
Jesus is Lord! He takes the highest station.

His Strength Made Perfect

Vain thoughts, Oh Lord, appealingly,
    If I could from my weakness now be free;
Yet I must own, deep mystery,
    The path of life in full I cannot see.
The whole is only known to thee;
    What kindness draws the veil so lovingly;
Unanswered prayer it could not be,
    For no good thing, will You withhold from me!
What patience waits so tenderly;
    And takes my hand, so firm, so faithfully.
Will You, by Your own company,
    Dear Saviour, help me still, to follow Thee.
To wait awhile on bended knee,
    And know that there is all-sufficiency;
Your grace for my humanity.
    Maybe, dear Father, I shall plainly see,
With all my earthbound frailty;
    Then is Your strength made mine so perfectly!

Pressing Towards the Mark

One thing, Oh Lord, do You require,
    And this one thing would I desire,
My Lord, to trust in Thee:
    It seems of royal consequence;
Of providential recompense;
    A heart at rest in Thee:
Oh land of God, there I would dwell;
    Place, where my Lord, 'Immanuel',
Seen at the table of the Lord:
    Transfigured now this earthly board.

Oh for a single heartedness;
    A mind of lowly humbleness,
Where I delight in Thee:
    Meaner attractions crucified;
Ambition by Him sanctified:
    That He delightsome be.
This would my heart, now recognise;
    Follies of earth, let me despise:
This your desire, Oh heart of mine,
    Accept God's gift and make Him thine!

What of the way, that I must take?
    What of life's journey, I must make?
This I commit to Thee!
    As I commit, Lord, help me trust,
You know my frame, it is but dust;
    May prayer my recourse be:
What You begin You will perfect,
    None of my needs will You neglect;

Lord, will You help me understand,
    Accepting all from Your dear hand!

Not by the effort of my hands,
    Can I fulfill Your love's demands;
Lord, let me gaze at Thee:
    And yet my heart so often sees -
Alternative's apparent ease.
    And yet, so patiently:
In love, You ask Your child "to wait,"
    Knowing that God is never late!
It seems that wrong will have its day:
    But love will trace a better way!

About Prayer

Lord Teach Us How To Pray

Lord Jesus, as we see You pray,
    Somehow we feel, this is the way;
That we must take, for every day,
    Your love constrains our hearts to say:
"We want close by Your heart to stay,
    And at Your feet our burdens lay;
To rise, just like the sun's first ray,
    Which ends the night and clears away,
The shadows, lest our feet should stray,
    From that sweet place we saw You pray."

"Our Father"

Father, within this sacred place,
    We lift our hearts and hands, and face;
Father, by right of all the race,
    But Father best of all by grace:
It is to You the way we trace,
    We need the throne of heavenly grace;
Each hindrance, Lord, will You displace,
    And all our unbelief erase:
That our weak faith may grow apace,
    Until we see You face to face.

"Who Art In Heaven"

We pray for help to understand,
    Where Jesus is, at God's right hand;
He sits on His established throne,
    And prays for those who are His own:
We wait His glory thus to share,
    For answered is His every prayer,

Our Great High Priest for us has died,
    And none who trust will be denied;
Our Advocate, once crucified
    And those He called, He justified.

"Hallowed Be Thy Name"

Lord, woe is me, with lips unclean,
    If I Your name should thus demean;
To hear the world blaspheme - what shame,
    To saints, so sacred, that dear name!
Lord of my tongue, for every word,
    Spoken on earth, in heaven is heard;
May all my speech thus seasoned be,
    Words that bring glory, Lord, to Thee:
Help me to use that name to win,
    Save me, dear Lord, from verbal sin.

"Thy Kingdom Come"

Did I forget, dear Lord, to pray,
    That I might bring one soul today?
Words are just words if I don't take,
    The gospel forth, for Jesus' sake.
When will Your Church, Lord, learn to ask?
    When will Your Church fulfil its task?
Help us rise up and meet this hour,
    Filled by Your passion and Your power,
To earth's remotest corner fling,
    The gospel, then bring back the King.

"Thy will be done"

That night in dark Gethsemane,
    We find Christ in an agony!

His sweat, are drops of blood, we see !
    And now we hear Him make this plea -
"Father, remove this cup from Me!"
    On yonder hill I see a Tree,
Ah, soul of mine, it was for thee:
    "Your will, not mine be done," cried He,
Take my will too, and let it be,
    Surrendered here at Calvary.

"On earth as it is in heaven"

Dear Lord, we've broken all Your laws;
    Few will defend a godly cause:
Then from Your word we walk away;
    Right is unpopular today.
In trouble, Lord, 'tis You we blame,
    We honour not Your holy Name;
Yet sure as waters fill the sea,
    The earth with glory full will be:
Dear Lord, the battle will be won,
    And here on earth Your will be done.

"Give us today our daily bread"

Lord, You have bidden us to pray,
    For bread, on which to feed today;
Help us to trust and simply say,
    "Thank You, dear Lord, just for the way,
Our every need has been supplied,
    And no good thing has been denied."
Remember those whose needs are great,
    For some, today will be too late:
Better a frugal meal to share,

And demonstrate a Christ-like care.

"Forgive Us Our Trespasses"

"Father, forgive", the Saviour said,
    Before He bowed His wounded head:
"Forgive your brother, lest it be,
    Forgiving grace withheld from thee."
Lord, for my sin You bore the blame,
    Let me not use another name;
For sins which deeply wounded Thee,
    That I from sin may be set free;
Freely forgive, then let it be,
    Father in heaven, forgiving me.

"Lead us not into Temptation"

Oh, dearest Saviour, just to know,
    You were no stranger to the foe;
Oh Son of Man, Oh world of woe:
    The tempter's rage, why was it so?
But You endured that we might know,
    There is a place where we may go,
And let our Conqueror overthrow,
    And to the adversary show,
That grace can like a river flow,
    In which a tempted saint may grow!

"Deliver Us From Evil"

The Serpent's bruise, The Saviour's heel;
    Oh, wounded head, so shall you feel,
Christ, manifested to destroy,
    And take your universal toy:
Let Him for ever cause your death,

    No more to blast your evil breath:
    Oh roaring beast, dark angel light,
        Then shall your morning be your night,
    Then in those moments you shall know,
        When vanquished in your overthrow!

"For Thine Is The Kingdom"

No other King, no other throne!
    No other Glory - His alone!
No other Prophet, Priest or King!
    No other Praise, but His to bring!
No other Shepherd, Saviour, Friend!
    No other Love, where spirits blend!
No other Advocate on high!
    No other Son of God to die!
No other Cross to set me free!
    No other hope of heaven but He!

"For Thine Is The Power"

Lord, at Your throne we bow the knee,
    The throne of all authority!
Yet in Your gracious sovereignty,
    Your grace has made a way for me!
All power is given unto Thee,
    And you have promised faithfully,
To all who love Your Calvary:
    Who, risen with Christ victoriously!
Then they may all partakers be,
    Of Your indwelling powerfully!

"For Thine Is The Glory"

The glory, Lord, will always be,
    Forever, Christ, bestowed on Thee:
But, Oh the glory of the 'Tree';
    The glory of Your Calvary!
Worthy the Lamb upon His throne!
    From where He reigns within His own!
Your glory, Lord, I can't define!
    Never, oh never, will it be mine:
Your love - Your power will ever shine,
    The glory, Lord, forever Thine!

"Forever and ever"

My years, dear Lord, are quickly done,
    Upon my days, Oh setting Sun:
For life's brief span, when once begun,
    Such is the race I lost or won.
My days and hours I give to Thee!
    Be Lord of life's dear destiny!
What love is this, divinest Friend?
    What grace is this that will extend?
What power, that will Your own defend?
    Oh Christ, Your Kingdom has no end!

"Amen"

Amen, Oh Lord, so let it be,
    Then will You give sweet rest to me?
To follow so obediently,
    To gaze at You so trustingly:
To wait for You so patiently,
    To serve You, Oh so faithfully!

All my fresh springs are found in Thee,
   In You is all my certainty,
My glory and eternity,
   Amen, dear Lord, so let it be.

A Birthday Prayer

There's nothing will give me
   More pleasure today,
Than to send you best wishes,
   For a happy birthday;
Then to tell you I paused
   For a while just to pray,
That all would be well
   As you go on your way.
I asked for God's love,
   On this wonderful day,
I asked that His grace
   Would be with you alway;
I prayed that His presence,
   Forever would stay,
Bringing joy and deep peace
   That will not pass away.
"There's a place near My heart"
   Is what I heard Him say,
May today be for you
   A happy birthday!

A True Heart Cry

    Just longing, Lord!
That longing lies within the heart,
It often knows not where to start.
And all who share the lonely part,
Where tears alone relieve the heart,
But trusting You will not depart,
    Just longing, Lord!
    Just longing, Lord!

    Just seeking, Lord!
Yes, sometimes seeking in the light,
The way is clear, the outlook bright,
The lanes of life laugh with delight,
Yes, sometimes groping in the night,
When senses search for sounds and sight,
    Just seeking, Lord!
    Just seeking, Lord!

    Just asking, Lord!
So many scorn the questing sigh,
"Tis but for us to do and die",
But then to know that in the sky,
Is One, Who on the cross asked "Why?"
Oh, Son of Man, pray hear my cry,
    Just asking, Lord!
    Just asking, Lord!

    Just praying, Lord!
Not always the deep yearning plea;
Arising when on bended knee,
In spirit to Your arms I flee,

Unuttered words to bring to Thee,
To know You'll understand and see,
    Just praying, Lord!
    Just praying, Lord!

Just coming, Lord!
Aware that I have nought to bring,
That only to a cross dare cling,
But I am coming to my King,
To find a refuge 'neath His wing,
Abiding, resting, sheltering,
    Just coming, Lord!
    Just coming, Lord!

Just singing, Lord!
How lovely here, to learn the song,
The song of those who do belong,
To Him, Who will right every wrong,
The Captain of a conquering throng
The One Whose grace has tuned my tongue,
    Just singing, Lord!
    Just singing, Lord!

What are You Trying to Say, Lord?

One thing my soul would ask of Thee,
    What hast Thou, Lord, to say to me?
As from the active ways of life,
    From scenes of battle and of strife,
My soul would turn to hear Thy voice.
    A weary heart will then rejoice,

Yet, Oh my God, while I would seek,
    While I would pray, Lord, will You speak?
My quest is but a little part,
    Of the great surging of Thy heart,
You would my rapt attention gain,
    Could I from lesser things refrain,
I pray no silent shadow cast,
    But, Oh my Lord, 'twas You spoke last,
Lord, will You tune my inward ear,
    And silence sounds that interfere,
I understand that Your best ways,
    Are found not in the strident days,
Not in the heaving of the earth,
    Is seen the Saviour's secret worth,
Not in the roaring of the gale,
    Will God unfold the untold tale,
Not in the fiery burning blast,
    Like words in iron's molten cast,
Ah! Sacred silences, Your choice,
    'Tis there I hear the still small voice,
One thing my soul would ask of Thee,
    What hast Thou, Lord, to say to me?

I Can't But You Can

Please help me, Lord, to bring to You,
    The things I simply cannot do,
And in the weakness of that hour,
    To prove the greatness of your power.

Then show me, Lord, from day to day,
    The throne of grace where I must pray,
Please may I see You reigning there,
    Available to answer prayer.

With limitations ever mine,
    So limitless Your power divine,
You are the God of vale and hills,
    You are the God of miracles.

Lord of my weakness, I would choose,
    My weakness in Your power to lose,
Your power is Your authority,
    Your power is my ability.

Thus may my mind contented be,
    A heart that trusts, Oh Lord, in Thee,
When nothing more that I can do,
    Then nothing, Lord, too hard for You!

Morning Prayer

Love You, Lord Jesus,
But help me today,
Help me to please You
In all that I say.
Your will is so safe,
To know it I pray,
Oh give me the grace
To do things Your way.

Waiting To Worship

Avoid the late and hurried pace,
How wise to leave,
A breathing space,
As you bow your head,
To seek Christ's face;
And present your soul,
To the throne of grace.

If your weary frame needs Christ's
Touch to find,
May your heart be at peace,
God is good and kind !
Let God's quiet calm,
Still your busy mind.
Understand that your life,
Is by love entwined.

Is your Christian life a loving thing?
Whatever God takes,
Are you willing to bring,
To the altar of Christ,
As an offering?
"Master, speak, for Your,
Servant is listening."

Bless the shepherd who seeks,
Your servant to be.
Bless my brothers,
And, Oh my God, bless me!

A Praying Christian

I've wondered long what I can do,
   In this bewildering hour for you;
There are no words which can explain,
   Just how I understand your pain:
The burden weighing on you now,
   I see, for sorrow scars your brow;
But I recall there is a place,
   It is the throne of heavenly grace:
May I assure you lovingly,
   I will pray for you faithfully,
I trust it helps to feel I care,
   But this I know, God answers prayer.

What are You Saying, Lord?

Lord, I'm to turn aside, You say,
   From things that happen every day,
The usual paths, the well-worn way,
   And e'en the place where oft I pray,
The scenes that laugh, so grand, so gay,
   Those valley times, where skies are grey,
Familiar track, how could I stray?
   Ah, Presence dear, Thy priceless ray,
Oh, cross, where I would seek to stay,
   Blessed Master, of the day to day?

By Prayer and Supplication

There is a way where God is real,
That way I want to go;
The throne of grace, there I must kneel:
For God ordained it so.

Those moments, Lord, not of distress,
Should answers be delayed;
But let me in that hour confess:
Lord, thank You that I prayed.

His eyes are never closed by sleep,
He'll never turn away;
He knows how best His child to keep:
And loves to hear them pray.

Prayer Leaps the Barrier of Miles

A long day O'er, the journey done,
    The parting, oh beloved one,
May He Who guards, both you and me,
    Grant us His peace, though we may be,
Parted, with many a mile between,
    Yet to us both, God's love is seen.
Through the long watches, of the night,
    May He, to Whom, all time is light,
Answer my prayer, thus comforting,
    And keep you safe, beneath His wing,
Blessed be He, Who leads the way,
    The Guide of life, from day to day.

God has prepared, and God has planned,
    Lord, You arrange, and understand,
Help us to live, as though this day,
    Could bring the news, "Christ on the way",
Should we turn, to the left or right,
    Or from God's best, stray out of sight.
Oh God, I ask, that Your dear voice,
    Will be the guide, of every choice,
One thing we know, that no mistake,
    A child of Thine, will overtake,
Lord, we can hide, no thing from You,
    In what we think, or say, or do.
Grant that the love, which bade us "come",
    Will be the love, that brings us home.

Oh, To Touch You

Oh to touch You, dear Lord Jesus
Just to know Your healing power
Let Your risen life, Redeemer
Be my life this very hour.

Will You touch me, loving Healer
Touch me with Your healing hands
In Your name, Oh Christ my Saviour
At the throne of grace I stand.

May my hand, Oh Mediator
Stretching out in love to You,
Could it be faith's great rewarder
That Your hand is stretched out, too?

Hand in hand with Christ my Shepherd
I will follow, You must lead,
By green pastures, by still waters
You know best just what I need.

Oh, my Christ, have You not promised
Hidden life, has God not planned
Christ and I together dwelling
In the hollow of God's hand?

Oh to touch You, Oh to touch You
Precious Lord, Who died for me,
Oh to see Your lovely radiance
Blessed Saviour, Oh touch me.

My Morning Dew

In the early hours of morning,
I would ask of Thee, my Lord,
May today I walk with Jesus,
Trusting in His faithful word.
Grant, that no worldly distraction,
Turn my gaze from His dear face,
May He occupy me fully,
As I learn to grow in grace.

Dear Lord Jesus, may Your Spirit,
Touch my heart afresh just now,
Let the morning dew of heaven,
Settle on my waking brow.
Save me, Lord, from barren moments,

Make this channel clean, I pray,
Wash me, Oh refreshing Fountain,
Teach me, Lord, teach me Thy way.

Thus available for service,
Should it be, "So send I you",
In that hour, Oh loving Master,
Let Your love come shining through.
Lord, I need a new outpouring,
Of Your all-sufficient grace,
Will You grant to me this blessing,
Will You let me see Your face?

Oh My Father

My Father, may Your blessing,
   Be with me, through this day;
Just to know that You will guide me,
   Along the Pilgrim Way:
While in precious conversation,
   My heart attuned with Thine;
Will You come and reassure me,
   I am Yours and You are mine:
Then let me seek Your love's consent,
   On everything I do;
And hear, "That as my Father has,
   Sent Me, so send I you!"

The Early Morning Dew

    Oh divine and holy presence,
    Will You stay right by my side
    In the early hours of morning
    Precious dew of God applied.
    Will You lead me to those pastures,
    Where the grass is green and wide,
    By a river full of water
    Shall my soul be satisfied.

    In the pressures of my morning
    Oh, my soul, be calm and still,
    Seeking guidance for my sharing
    Let me do my Master's will.
    May Your word like polished silver,
    Priceless gems, Oh grant me skill;
    Holy Spirit, please prepare me,
    My commission to fulfil.

Open! On the Godward Side

    Lord, for a while as I sit alone,
        Quietly to bow at Your loving throne;
    Best I know how to humbly pray,
        I've opened my heart to You today.
    All-seeing eye, You alone can see;
        Whether one part remains closed to Thee:
    With all my heart this prayer I would bring,
        Search me, Oh God, and take every thing -

Every thing, Lord, that could share a part;
    Swing open wide the door of my heart:
Oh, Holy Spirit fill to the brim,
    Then shall my life bring glory to Him.

Seasons

Birthdays are Milestones

    Milestones along life's trackless way,
        Are times to pause, look up and say;
    "Thank You", to Him Whose love each day,
        Has promised at your side to stay.
    My Father, I ask on this birthday,
        "Help me to love You, and trust, and pray:
    I place my hand in Your hand today,
        And ask for a light lest I should stray.
    Before You, Lord Jesus, the future I lay,
        And pray for Your presence and peace alway".

New Year Aspirations

Pray, take Your place, Lord, at my side,
    The old year ends, thus turns the tide,
What may I say for grace is wide,
    And ask that more grace be applied.
My Lord, please make Yourself more room,
    Should there be present any gloom,
Where self-life lurks, make it a tomb,
    Oh, loving Christ-life may there bloom,
Within this human soul of mine,
    Christ's fragrant presence, so Divine,
Lord, let it be a lovelier shrine,
    Where less of mine means more of Thine.
You were the Victor Who O'ercame,
    To do so, Lord, You bore my shame,
And now to use that lovely Name,

  Yet still it sets the heart aflame.
You wrestled with temptation's power,
  You struggled in that awful hour,
That You might be the Christian's tower;
  Your soldier, Captain, should not cower,
Nor should he ever turn his back,
  Though dark the day, though night be black,
Oh hand of mine, be never slack,
  For no resource does God's child lack.

Memories of Mother

Another year has come and gone,
And time itself has swiftly sped;
It hardly seems so many years:
Since Mother wiped away my tears.
While at her knees she gently led;
My falt'ring prayers, when said and done:
She kissed my lips and calmed my fears,
Her tender hand upon my head;
The other hand held mine in hers:
How lovely were those lovely years!

But many years have come and gone,
I laid my hand upon her head;
And kissed her lips, then she passed on.
That angel now is gently led,
To living streams, to living bread;
I cannot think of her as dead:
The Shepherd holds her lovely hand,

And leads her to her home so grand.
With passing time, maybe I'll stand:
Mother and I in Gloryland!

When all the years have come and gone,
And time's long ages are all done;
The fight of faith is fought and won:
Won, too, the race long since begun.
One day I'll see my Saviour's face,
Re-union blessed by His embrace;
Please God, I'll turn to see the place:
Where stands that angel pure through grace.
My childhood faith, sweet loving care,
With Christ, because of Mother's prayer!

Abiding Security

If ought should dim the certainty,
    Dear Lord, that You are near to me:
When sight has ceased to satisfy;
    And reason rises to ask "Why?"
For fear, e'en faith would fluctuate,
    Thus falling foul of Satan's hate.
Lord, should I lose my grasp of You,
    Could this great fact come shining through!
My hope of heaven does not depend;
    Nor need my destiny defend:
The thought, what human arrogance;
    That O'er the course of life's distance:
These feeble fingers fixed to all,

That I call 'God', but must I fall?
Ah! human arm though e'er so strong:
    To you it never did belong;
The fact of faith's security;
    Not me, but Oh my God, in Thee.
Lord, let not e'en the thought be found,
    That I may stand - presumptuous ground!
But that my heart at rest may be -
    Amazing grace has hold of me!

Infant Wonderful

Prophets spoke with great delight;
    Angels sang one starry night:
Thus may I with all my might;
    Celebrate that sacred sight:
Little Lamb, lo! let Your light;
    Shine, thus shall the world be bright:
Son of God, all wrongs make right;
    Blessed be Him, Whose fearless flight:
Penetrates His people's plight.

Monarch of the Manger

He's the Monarch of the Manger,
He's the Babe of Bethlehem;
He's the Christ of yonder Cradle:
He's the Man among earth's Men.
He's the Saviour in the Stable,

He's the Sovereign in the Stall;
He's the Grace of Heaven and Glory:
He's the Almighty Lord of All!

Oh Bethlehem

The Centuries Have Passed, Oh Bethlehem;
   Prophet's Inspired Forecast, "Peace For Men":
His Name Is "Prince Of Peace", Oh Manger;
   But To This Grace Am I A Stranger?
A Legacy Of Peace, Thou "Son Of Man";
   Oh Cross, Release The Peaceful Plan:
Passed Understanding, Mary's Child;
   Angelic Singing, "A Heart By Peace Made Mild."

The Day Star

I see a star on distant far horizon,
   Its light all other stars does far outshine;
My life drawn onward by its great attraction:
   To worship there at Bethlehem's lowly shrine.
Shine on! Shine on! Oh guiding star that leads the way,
   Oh may my eyes look upward to the sky;
Please may I come, in trust to where the Saviour lay:
   Once more to wonder, while my longing soul asks "why"?

A baby, oh a babe! Whose lovely form divine,
   His manger-cradle may I worship there?
Yet, as I gaze, those eyes so pure are raised to mine:
   And then to touch Him with a humble prayer.
How can it be, that God Himself became a man?
   To walk the human road, what mystery;
To live my life and die my death, how great the plan:
   The plan of love which loves the world and yet loves me.
I hear sweet strains; a throng of angel voices,
   All heaven in harmony for joy does sing;
What glad new sounds as 'glory' thrills with praises:
   For born today is Jesus Christ the King.
Sing! Sing! Ye choirs, your song must fill eternity,
   Oh tell the world its Saviour has been born;
Sing on! Sing on! Your glad news spread O'er land and sea:
   The song of love, and joy, and peace; and hope's grand dawn.
Oh Bethlehem, what mighty 'Love' is cradled there!
   Oh little Babe, what joys enshrined in Thee;
"Peace, perfect peace", passed understanding, Virgin's child:
   A day of hope, "Amen, so let it be"!
Ring out, Oh bells! Ring out with mighty pealing!
   While heavenly trumpets sound throughout the sky!
Let all creation rise with jubilation:
   A babe is born, the King of Kings, and Lord Most High!

God's Passover Lamb

Blessed Lamb, most precious blood:
    Ah! Night of judgement and of wrath;
O'er alien powers there stood,
    Wrath's messenger - but let his path:
'Pass over', there the sign;
    Let it alone distinguish they,
Within love's grand design;
    Prepare for God, love's greater day.

Thus sent, they now prepare,
    As Christ's great Passover drew nigh;
For there God's Lamb must share,
    This frugal feast before He die:
The Lord, with great desire,
    Sat down to share with those He chose;
Soon to be lifted higher,
    Yet they this feast must not dispose.

Until in Kingliness,
    When at My Father's own right hand;
I stand in glorious dress:
    Till then, not I, but this command.
This bread, not mine to share;
    But celebrate in memory:
So often thus shall you prepare,
    This feast remembering Me.

Those trembling lips that spoke,
    What gentle hands that held the bread;
With given thanks He broke:
    Then, those He loved He fed.
Oh cup! Oh testament of blood,
    Unworthy, yet may I;
Remembering Him, Who wholly good:
    Once came for me to die.

In shadowed agony,
    Only divinest lips could bring;
With sorrowing harmony:
    If only I had heard them sing.
Echoes, I hear them yet,
    Yet, other echoes could it be;
But see, it is to Olivet:
    And then Gethsemane!

The Master turns to speak,
    Stay here, My brothers, stay and pray;
Lest trial find you weak:
    And then I see Him walk away.
Never to sorrow's sight,
    Unique the scene before their eyes;
He struggled there that night:
    What agony, my God, what cries!

Preciousness Poured Out

Home at beloved Bethany,
    Where, on His way to Calvary;
My Lord, I see so fragrantly,
    Ah! Let me weep awhile for Thee;
Mary, her love for Christ so strong,
    Her deed to meaner souls so wrong.

No lesser sacrifice could make,
    The quest fulfilled for His dear sake;
Never her Lord would she forsake:
    Her only treasure, gently break;
As precious ointment now poured forth,
    Token of Jesus' precious worth.

Most blessed place at Jesus' feet,
    Where love is costly yet complete;
Here, love will constantly repeat:
    Love never fails - thus no defeat;
Love Him! Then choose a lowly place,
    Where love can gaze into Love's face!

The Lord Turned and Looked

Oh, eyes divine, I see them turn,
    On Calvary's eve, so dark a day.
Yet, heart of Christ, that once did yearn,
    You look at heaven and then You pray.
Ah, gracious gaze, could I but learn;
    Let me just catch that treasured ray:
Could I now know that love does burn;
    Prayer is Your life! Love is Your way!

About the Suffering of Jesus

I prayed afresh to understand,
The Cross my Lord did bear;
I asked if I could see the hands,
That cruel nails did tear!

I asked if I could see the face,
The loveliest face of all;
Then, could I stand upon that place,
Where sweat like blood did fall!

What of those pillars where they tied,
Your gentle hands and feet;
My Lord, all mercy was denied,
No tongue could e'er repeat!

Lord, may I look, that wound, Your side,
Perhaps Your heart to see;
Is there a place where I may hide,
Oh heart, which broke for me!

No tongue could tell, no heart may feel,
The depth of Jesus' woe;
Nor shall I ever understand,
My Lord, why did You go?

Why did You go? Oh, tell me why?
Those thorns upon Your head;
Find me a place where I may cry,
You suffered in my stead!

What mystery, they bow the knee,
What blows they aimed at You;
They spit - they cry blasphemously,
Lord, shall I ever know?

Ah, weary One, beneath the weight,
Along the Calvary Road;
Oh place, outside the City Gate,
The Cross an awful load!

I hear those cries which rent the skies,
Worst agony of all;
As God, to His own Son denies,
Himself! Oh desolate call!

"My God, my God, forsaken, Why?
Your face is turned away"
No other cry could rend the sky;
As on that awful day!

The Lamb of God Who knew no sin,
For me, He sin became;
He died my guilty soul to win,
For me, bore all the blame!

I was not there, Lord, when You died,
And yet 'twas plain to see;
Two arms of love were opened wide,
Yes, opened wide for me.

By grace one day I'll hold that hand,
To find those wounds remain;
They are, e'en in Immanuel's Land,
A record of His pain!

Oh Way, by Whom we come to God,
No other way can save;
Oh fountain, filled with Jesus' blood,
Oh hope, beyond the grave!

Oh Lamb of God, I come, I come,
I must keep coming, Lord;
No other way to heaven and home,
Dear Lord, this is Your word!

I prayed afresh to understand,
The sufferings of my Lord;
Then can I question if He planned,
To take me at my word!

My Child, Behold My Hands

Oh child of Mine, behold My hands,
    And see your name engraven there:
Beloved one, behold My hands,
    The marks of My affliction where;
I proved My love for you, My child:

Then may you simply understand,
When all seems furious and wild;
    Within the hollow of My hand,
Your life is hid with Christ in God:
    One thing, My child, I ask of you,
To trust the hand that holds the rod;
    Omnipotence can all things do.
My hands are there but trust must place,
    Faith's everything, whole and complete;
Then prove My all-sufficient grace,
    While resting at Your Saviour's feet.

A Living Lord Jesus

Behind closed doors they trembled,
    Those ten men so filled with dread;
They had spent three years with Jesus,
    They had seen the hungry fed:
He had loved the little children,
    Laid His hand on many a head;
His word had mastered wind and storm:
    Those feet the waves did tread.

Sad memory, could they forget,
    The sound of hatred in their tread;
That multitude with swords and clubs,
    A violent column; at its head:
One of their number who betrayed,
    The sign, a kiss, and then they led:
The Lord away to suffer shame;

Then to the cross His blood to shed.

But when He needed them the most,
    They forsook the Lord and fled;
It seemed that one would break his heart:
    His Lord had turned, no word was said.
The cock had crowed, his tears had flowed,
    Could he forget those eyes that pled;
But, Oh! three times, "I know Him not";
    He failed his Lord, his Lord was dead.

Another, with bewildered love,
    Recalled some words from yonder tree;
Sweet tender care, the one who bear:
    A spear had torn His side, but she,
The sword had pierced her own soul, too,
    "Beloved Disciple, I to thee;
My Mother lend", thus would he tend:
    Calvary's assignment just for me.

To where He lay, e' er break of day,
    One went, but Him she could not see;
"Oh, they have taken Him away",
    So strange, how could it really be?
The two had been to see the tomb,
    While Mary wept so bitterly:
Grave cloths are folded carefully;
    But where was Christ, Oh where was He?

She stooped to stare, so clearly there,
    While weeping broken-heartedly;
The rock their seat, at head and feet:
    Two angels, Oh how radiantly,

"Woman, we pray, why weep today?"
    At rest in death so recently:
I know not where they have laid Him;
    Taken is He but Lord to me!

She could not know or understand,
    Glancing, she saw one standing there;
He saw her grief and asked her, "Why?"
    Through tears she saw a gardener's care,
"His sacred body I will take,
    But tell me, tell me, tell me where?"
"Mary", was all the Master said;
    Turning, she saw Him standing there.

Then in a moment all was changed,
    Saddened with grief and dark despair;
The doors were shut and locked, indeed:
    But suddenly their Lord was there,
Forlorn and hopeless, men bereaved,
    Now here He is, His form so fair:
He is alive! He is alive!
    The thrill of peace took wings on air.

His peace He shared, what peace is this?
    Peace, risen Lord, What can compare?
His hands He showed and then His side:
    Scars, which a Saviour's love declare.
Healer of wounds but not His own,
    They must remain for ever there;
Transition - time to eternity:
    Wounded, but glory He will share.

Ten men were sad, ten men are glad!
    Let none their sorrow thus despise;.
The Cross does well to break the heart:
    But hail the day that saw Him rise!
The Lord of death, is Lord of life,
    Blessed be those apostolic eyes:
They saw, but we must wait awhile;
    Oh certain hope, faith's glad surprise.

Two men were absent from that room,
    The hand that held the silver prize;
The traitor's kiss; no heart that loved:
    We shall not see him in the skies.
Doubting disciple, where was he?
    Whose unbelief could not disguise:
He was not there; he missed his Lord;
    To watch, and wait, and trust how wise.

My Lord, my God, this grand confession,
    Faith's second chance, so often true;
Oh, great commission, "As My Father:
    Has sent Me, so send I you",
Then the Lord of earth and heaven,
    Breathed on them, His breath like dew:
"Take My gospel of forgiveness;
    This promised power enabling you".

On the day of resurrection,
    A country road - disciples, two;
Sad, bewildered conversation:
    Until alongside Jesus drew,
From the Scriptures, Great Expounder,

All that was said concerning You:
With burning hearts, the journey over;
   While breaking bread, at once they knew.

Living Saviour, thus to heaven,
   You returned Your work to do;
Pleading for us – interceding:
   That home of many mansions, too,
May I kneel, now, at Your footstool,
   Oh, Lamb of God, will You endue:
Your living, loving, gentle Spirit;
   To make me more and more like You.

Ponderings & Musings

A More Excellent Way

To those within the bond of love,
Parting is pain, for love does bind;
Yet it must be, for life is life:
But hearts in love are intertwined!

The author of true love is God,
Love's questing feet, with heaven are shod;
Alternate origin but none:
For God is love and love is God!

Inferior types, could there be such,
Are substitutes, sad certainty;
Oh inner infidelity:
Sad consequence, true tragedy!

"Love never fails", Divinest heart!
Oh love of God, eternal ray;
Earth's oceans have their boundary:
But love, how excellent a way!

Oh love, my love, true love must pray,
"Maintain within this sacred flame;
Construct a mirror, that love's life:
Reflect the radiance of Your Name."

To love, no distance is too far,
The longest length, true love can leap;
It spans the barrier of miles!
And cannot fail to care and keep.

Love prays, prepares, preserves and pays,
Perceive its purpose, precious heart;
It pauses, practices and plans:
In partnership pursues its part.

Nothing destroys this holy state,
For partnership, eternity;
Where love of each, for each loves God:
For God is love's blessed destiny!

But let love grow, its heart expand,
Enlarging love's capacity;
For love in loving must improve:
Increasing giving quality.

Question love's grand priority,
Does it defy all gravity?
All lower than divinity:
Infringes love's sweet purity.

Dare death's dread doom, destroy dear love,
Love's interchange, would then be hate;
Will love in life have unity:
Then lie discarded at heaven's gate?

The bridal love, a hallowed type,
Of Christ, Himself, the church His bride;
Can Jordan separate this state?
Would heaven be heaven, with love denied?

At one with Christ, forever one,
For what can separate this state?
At Calvary love's union, done:
Or was the cross, for love, too late?

Thine altar, love would take its stand,
Its glad bequest, supremacy;
Love's author grips the yielding hand:
Oh gracious love, this love for me!

Oh Love in Heaven, my Advocate,
My Great High Priest, Oh Son of Man;
My Shepherd guards His sheepfold gate:
To snatch His sheep, no other can.

Love's abiding life is sharing,
Just as the branch is to the vine;
Then love's precious fruit is bearing:
His life flowing out through mine.

Love in heaven, forever caring,
His was the love that first loved me;
Guard the one Your love is sharing:
That both beneath love's wings might be.

Lord, Your love, the love that called me,
Into love's fellowship with You;
Be the grace that keeps me near Thee:
With Jesus only, in full view!

An Open Heart

>My heart is open to Thee, Lord,
>   Like flowers the sun embrace;
>I long to feast upon Thy word,
>   I long to see Thy face!

For the Conversion of St Paul

I met Him on the Damascus Road;
My guilty past, a crushing load!
I hated the 'Name'! It was like a flame!
That fired my anger to fiercest heat!

To terrify them, who followed the feet!
Of a Galilee Man, a Carpenter - Crucified!
Who went about doing good, and died,
Like a villain who dies for his deeds!

He pleaded as One, Who aware of my needs!
Cast a light, thus scorching my sight!
And in my disgrace, as I lay on my face,
I did hear, what seemed to appear ...

A voice, which in gentle tone,
Asked me, "Why did I ever condone,
Such passion and hatred for Him, Who alone,
Had died to atone, to make all His own?"

My heart was broken, and I found I had spoken;
The Name I had hated!
I asked of the Lord, Who He was? And then waited,
He told me, "My name is Jesus."

Grace Did Much More Abound

Though a million tread the Calvary Road,
Then a million, million more;
The crimson flood will bear the load -

Oh, ocean, unfathomed floor!
Can God forget? Yes, a million times,
And a million O'er and O'er:
Though a million souls with a million crimes,
He'll remember them no more!

The Lane of Life

When love requited love's advance,
Launching a life on circumstance;
Not some celestial prominence:
Producing pearls in eminence.
But co-humanity has flung,
Into the lane of life its young.

Shielded and safe by stage by stage,
Progress is portrayed page by page;
Care in creation, yet with pain:
The body grows, the lung, the brain.
The heart, then is the human whole,
Nay! It must see the sacred soul.

What of the welcome which awaits,
This child of time anticipates;
With mind untaught, yet how will thought:
Construct the babe who has been brought.
Into the complex choice of calls,
That echo from a thousand halls.

The kinder into kindness creeps,
Although in its first moment weeps;
Anxious await the early cry:
The lusty lung, the soundless sigh.
Yet she who smooths the downy hair,
Has counted with creative care.

Sad state, the one who comes too late,
Too late for love, thus closed the gate;
No fanfare sounds when you arrive:
Antipathy! It is alive!
The broken cord, but not of love,
Ah mercy! One beholds above.

Exposed! Thus winds the way, while wear,
The one will tear! The other care;
Omnipotence, take both and bring:
Flay every foe! Your fury fling!
Pray, pinions poise with pageantry!
And ambient ambitiously!

The Secret of the Shadows

Almighty God, give me the grace,
To dwell within "the secret place",
Yet though I may not see Your face,
Your shadow will my life embrace.
Oh loving Lord, my pathway trace;
Stay with me while I run the race:
Though seeing not, my doubts displace:
Glad day when shadows flee apace.

For a Daughter and Her Mum

Were ever two so dear to Him?
Was one as ever dear as He to you?
Was there a home where Christ within,
Brought love's new day of service warm and true?

A home where memory was gold!
Where kindness gave with lavish open hand!
What wealth was gleaned from wounds of old!
Transformed because it was the way He planned!

The place of prayer was always near,
One could not just rise up and go away.
Ah, lovely thought the Lord did hear,
And prayer was often answered on that day.

May Jesus be right by your side,
To bear the heavy load you carry now.
You will I know in Him confide:
I know His hand will smooth your anxious brow.

Sufficient grace, please God, each day,
For two who follow each step of the way!
So precious, Lord, are they to You!
Then tell me, that you'll gently see them through!

The Eye that Guides

Will You, my Lord, instructor be,
    Thus by Your Spirit teaching me?
Where e'er I go:
    I go with Thee and understand;
Your eye can see -
    Not to observe reproachfully;
    But just to guide so lovingly.

Simplicity

    Lord, grant me a life,
        that can demonstrate;
    With sincere simplicity:
        grant me a hope that,
    Beholds heaven's gate;
        with a childlike,
        Trust in Thee.

Sea - The Soul Mender

The grassy slope and rocky face,
The radiant sun and splendid space;
The cry of Gull, its echo wide,
The ebb and flow of sea and tide:
The search for God, Oh can it be,
Completed here, beside the sea?

The weary frame receiving healing,
The worried mind sweet rest is feeling;
The tortured soul discerns the meaning,
The love of God is gently stealing:
The search for peace, Oh can it be,
Completed here, beside the sea?

The air so pure, Oh Holy Spirit,
The slackened pace, Oh may its limit;
The grander view, perspective give it,
The re-commission, let me hear it:
The search for healing, let it be,
Completed here, beside the sea?

The seas of life and death passed over,
Earth's fear and failure gone for ever;
The gales of life can rage no longer,
The love of Christ has proved the stronger:
The quest for God, Oh let it be,
Completed there, beside that sea!

Cords and the Cross

Lord, what of the joys
    which are closely bound,
With a life that would
    take up the Cross?
And what of the cords,
    which are closely wound;
When for Thy sake,
    we count all things loss?

The Harbour

The harbour scene recalled today,
    Uncapturable thought!
Of time beyond the memory,
    To bring to birth one fought.
A little life was lightly launched,
    To whit with what purport,
Its sights not set, its sword not whet;
    What gallant sea life sought!

The wide-walled waters, where within,
    Scenes of serenity;
Fair fancy falsely feels secure,
    Were prison walls to be.
The toil of travail trace, too true,
    For no immunity;
Borne battered barques across the bar,
    Discerned by Deity.

The lights of the final harbour,
    Which beam eternal ray;
Have not flashed across the waters,
    That bear me on my way.
But the hand of my own Pilot;
    My guide of day to day,
Is waiting to catch my moorline,
    Anchored in Beulah's Bay.

A Royal Rest

> Oh, my Keeper, be the Guardian,
>   Of the sanctum of my heart.
> Grant that no discordant influence,
>   In my soul shall share a part!
> May Your peace possess me fully,
>   While Your quiet reigns within!
> Will You give to me the harmony:
>   Of the royal rest of heaven?

A Beautiful Life

> I ask for a beautiful life,
>   dear Lord;
> I seek for a heart that
>   can sing:
> I pray for a trust that accepts
>   Your word;
> I covet a place 'neath
>   Your wing.
>
> I ask to be shadowed beneath
>   the Cross;
> I seek for the smile of
>   Your face:
> I pray for a sight of Your wounds,
>   dear Lord;
> I covet yet more of
>   Your grace.

About Signposts

The path which leads to life, my friend,
    As sure as it will have an end:
So many a prayer your heart will send;
    Immunity - will not defend!
But grace abounding God will lend,
    And by His presence will attend;
All questing souls whose feet would tend,
    Towards Him on Whom all souls depend!

The way to life is well defined,
    And they who seek will surely find:
Imperative to have the mind;
    Of One Whose boundless love is kind!
A covenant in blood was signed,
    Yet enmity has undermined;
And alien powers have all combined,
    To make a pilgrim look behind!

It seems that God His will displays,
    If you would understand His ways:
To Him you've given all your days,
    Then listen with care to what He says.
Make Christ the object of your gaze,
    Confront with Bible truth each phase;
Let heaven observe, "Behold he prays":
    Despise not God-ordained delays.

But something I would ask of you:
    Though many a pilgrim's quest is true:
Yet some have other motives, too,
    They leave the way with signs too few.
Destructive work do they pursue,
    Others, the signs of God review;
And then invent their signposts new:
    What harm unfaithful souls can do!

Oh pilgrim to that city, fair,
    'Tis not enough to travel there:
While other sheep for whom I care;
    Are lost; bewildered by despair!
Once, signposts stood; now men cry, "Where?"
    Do not at ruins stand and stare;
My armour wear; My truth to bear:
    Go where those signposts need repair.

One day, the Guide of life will show,
    The journey which He ordered so:
The way you could not understand;
    You'll see, it was the way He planned.
Your Lord, He will make no mistake:
    He knows the way that you must take;
He'll always be right by your side,
    That you might lean upon your Guide.

Helping and Caring

How swiftly the moments are passing;
    History written - each tale is told:
The tale, are some pages still missing;
    From pages all edged with pure gold?

For some folk these pages are tarnished;
    Their deeds full of cruelty and shame,
Life's story, their object is anguish,
    No love because hate is their name!

For others, life means simply caring,
    To cheer and to love and to share;
Life's joy is in helping and bearing,
    The moment of need finds them there.

Life's mountains, Oh God, are for climbing,
    May I help my brother climb too;
The summit is only appealing,
    As I stand there my brother with you.

God is Love

When I think of all the promises,
    Oh God, that You have made;
When I recall the answers,
    To the prayers which I have prayed;
When I understand my Shepherd's care,
    Each time that I have strayed:
        Then I know that God is love!

Just by faith to find the Saviour,
    Hanging there on Calvary;
Just to feel my sins forgiven,
    For He paid my penalty;
Just abiding at the Cross,
    With its blessed shadow over me:
        Then I know that God is love!

There at God's right hand in heaven,
    Is the One Who pleads for me;
There in glory interceding,
    Christ's own present ministry;
There, a home of many mansions,
    Planned from all eternity:
        Then I know that God is love!

When my needs all pass before me,
    He has promised to provide;
When the way is rough and lonely,
    He is always at my side;
When the fury of the gale breaks,
    There's a place where I may hide:
        Then I know that God is love.

Whatever were my yesterdays,
    He will surely understand;
Whatever comes to me today,
    I would take from His dear hand;
Whatever life's tomorrow means,
    I'll know His heart has planned:
        Then I'll know that God is love!

About the Lord

Oh highest peak of Scripture inspiration,
Incarnate Word of God's Self-revelation;
Oh Son of God, Who takes the highest station,
Worshipped as Lord with loving adoration;
Servant and Saviour, what humiliation!

Oh Son of Man, You chose not reputation,
But meekly bore our human degradation;
As peers and prophets point in expectation,
Not as a law on Sinai's high location;
Engraved in stone but void of motivation.

Ah, Adam's sin - Oh world of desolation,
Because of you, from God, man's separation;
From Eden's grove to every generation,
All are concluded under condemnation;
Is there no hope of reconciliation?

No bright horizon of full reclamation,
Are we to sink in total desperation?
Oh love of God, what gracious condescension,
That mighty heart which beats with love's intention;
Planned for our race the wholeness of redemption.

God sent His son to purchase our salvation,
So perfectly was timed that intervention;
The cradle, to the cross His destination,
Atonement by God's Lamb, no complication;
Victorious in pain, love's grand devotion!

He was alone - for us no dereliction,
Dread depths of death, no terror's realisation;
But, Oh my God, what powers of resurrection,
Jesus is Lord with heaven's confirmation;
Christ's present place, what glorious acclamation!

But now His power, prevailing intercession,
Oh pleading Christ, transcendent advocation;
A home He now prepares, the presentation,
"Forever with the Lord," glorification!
Christ coming soon, ah! What anticipation!

To watch and wait, this do with preparation,
To work with Christ with yielded consecration;
To love Him, with love's grand and great obsession,
Let Amen" sound; eternity's duration;
Christ, King of kings, the hope of every nation!

A Home Christ Loved

There was a home at Bethany,
A home where Jesus loved to be;
No home is home unless that He,
Would grace it with His company:
What healing it may bring to thee,
And to your own dear family:
This is a prayer that constantly;
The Son of God will graciously,
Dwell in your home that all may see;
The love of God, so full, so free.

Light of the World

I was not there, Oh God, when holy eyes,
    Beheld a sight - a world in dark disguise;
I did not see Omnipotence arise:
    And from His throne, release light's swift surprise!
How come, this world, formless and void and dark?
    What circumstance - a tragedy so stark?
Whence, evil power, to leave so deep a mark?

Oh, Sun of Righteousness, with healing wing,
    Hail, gladdening morn', great light, arise and fling;
Aside that power of darkness, who did bring:
    So dark a night, with death a dreadful sting.
Oh, word of hope, in that rebellious hour,
    Bruised head; bruised heel; who with triumphant power;
Blest Cross, above the wrecks of time, to tower.

Light of the world, scatter our dark despair,
    Take Thou our hearts, Yourself, Oh radiance fair!
Ambassadors, the torch of Christ to share;
    Where darkness reigns to be your beacon there.
Then when life's darksome valley road we take;
    And when on Jordan's brink our footprint make:
Eternal Light, be ours as we awake.

Sir, the Well is Deep

Our Christ once walked the human road,
    Our Christ grew tired;
The Fountainhead of life itself,
    Water desired:
But when a soul in need drew near,
    His heart was fired;
Confronting customs, culture cruel,
    His grace inspired:
A self-disclosure of His life,
    She then inquired;
But gospel grace though given demands,
    The truth required:
Perfection of free grace and truth,
    By God admired.

Your well is deep, Oh living Lord,
    Oh Christ divine!
How then shall I a mortal draw,
    That Thine be mine?
Yet can it be, great mystery,
    That all of Thine;
Bequeathed by Thee, bestowed by Him,
    Through Whom You shine:
So large the love, so great the grace,
    Joy's gems so fine;
A peace so deep, a hope so strong,
    So safe its shrine:
Deep well, but at its Fountainhead,
    All may be mine.

My well is deep, thus would I come,
    Oh Lord to Thee;
A void so large I see within,
    'Eternity!'
To draw with, I have nothing, Lord:
    For not to me,
Is given the gift to satisfy;
    Sufficiently.
Oh Maker of the mould of man,
    Like unto Thee;
Designer of the human dawn,
    And destiny:
This well too deep for me, my Lord,
    But not to Thee.

To Look and Look at Him

To seek You, Lord, my Lord, just You,
    A sinner would His Saviour view:
To fix my eyes upon Your face;
    What radiancy, my Lord, what grace:
Beholding with unbroken gaze;
    Omnipotence, my Lord what ways.
Oh Spirit, will You not unveil,
    The One Whom You delight to hail:
Take from my sight all that may hide,
    For I would dwell in Jesus' side;
And look, and look, and look at Him;
    Then look, 'til all, all else grows dim!

The Master's Men

    The shadow of the Cross was long,
        It reached as far as Bethlehem;
    It marked the life of Him, so young,
        As God prepared His Son for them.
    For those - for whom - He came to die,
        Though that include all Adam's race;
    Dear Lord, now reigning 'there on high',
        At Calvary, You took my place.

    The shadowed life, the life of One,
        For thirty years the shadow cast;
    The hidden life of God the Son,
        But now, His ministry at last.
    'Neath Jordan's waters He must bend,
        The voice from heaven they, too, must hear;
    The Dove, the Spirit, God did send,
        "You are My well-loved Son, so dear".

    Oh Christ, I hear You calling men,
        To leave their all and follow Thee;
    They must observe Your life, and then,
        So taught, to understand the Tree.
    Where love's redeeming work was done,
        They, too, must see and understand;
    How souls are drawn, how men are won,
        How, Son of Man, Your path was planned.

    The life of love, disciples share,
        Through Christ was God revealed to them;
    Twelve men must see that 'Life' at prayer,
        The Fountainhead from which would stem:

Life of Divine simplicity,
    Feet that were with the gospel shod;
He, Who was perfect purity,
    Both, Son of Man and Son of God.

They knew the love, they saw the life,
    The life that raised men from the dead;
The life that calmed the mind of strife,
    That laid its hand upon the head:
When many a child to Him was brought,
    His Saviour-heart was opened wide;
"Suffer the little ones", He taught;
    And let them in My love abide.

His healing power, they saw Him touch,
    The fevered brow; the feeble frame;
No sickness ever proved too much,
    Such was the power of Jesus' name.
They saw Him calm the raging sea,
    They saw Him still the stormy soul;
He spoke the word, then let it be,
    His 'mission' was to make men whole.

The Lord is there at Olivet,
    With Him, His chosen company;
One of their number went to get,
    Betrayer, at the treasury.
"Deny You, Lord - not me - not me,"
    So say they all, but words are vain;
Sleeping, while He in agony,
    Unconscious of the Saviour's pain.

A brutal throng, the One to take,
    The One Whose love was all Divine;
The One Who everything did make,
    To suffering goes, this Saviour mine.
What of the ones through three short years,
    Disciples, whom the Lord had led;
What of the lonely Lamb, Whose tears,
    As they forsook their Lord, and fled.

A Sharing Christian

Bearing one another's burdens,
    Sharing a fellow traveller's load;
Simply helping one another,
    Companionship along life's road:
Reminding you of Jesus' love,
    His is a tried and trusted word;
So many tokens from above,
    Your anxious prayer His ear has heard;
At best I can be but a friend,
    But Christ is with you to the end!

Lord Jesus, What are You Doing?

I know my Sovereign Lord divine,
Is praying for this soul of mine;
He ever lives to intercede,
Because He understands my need.

Ah! Praying One, such mighty love,
That fills Your glorious courts above;
No limit can that love contain,
Yet, even me it can sustain.

Dear Lord, what of Your priceless worth?
Unrivalled throughout heaven and earth;
Your Father ever hears You pray,
And never will He answer, "Nay"

No name, Oh Christ, is lifted higher -
Than Yours, thus would my heart aspire;
To where You see Your Father's face,
Oh, blessed paradise of grace.

What of Your wounds, divinest Friend,
Scars which, though time, no healing lend;
Yet for Your child, so weak they plead,
As, Lamb of God, You intercede.

As Advocate, Oh Son of Man,
You plead, I need no other than,
The One, Who wore our human frame;
You bore our nature and our shame.

Our Great High Priest, You now appear,
And God His Son will always hear;
There was an altar where for me,
You paid the price and made me free.

I would live worthy of my Lord,
Shine, Holy Spirit, through His word;
Show me the throne, my dear Lord there,
He ever lives to plead in prayer.

Everything in His Hands

Jesus Christ, my King and Saviour,
    What a treasure, just to know;
That Your arms are round about me,
    All Your love to me You show.
Help me ne'er to lose the vision,
    Of the beauty which I see;
Where my eyes see Jesus only,
    Christ is everything to me.

Yes, the secret is to trust You,
    Leaning hard upon the Lord;
Lingering where, in that dear presence,
    There Your voice is clearly heard.
Faithful Friend, to all Your people,
    Through a fellowship of prayer;
"Bearing one another's burdens,"
    Sharing one another's care.

"As the eagle", great Protector,
    Hide Your own beneath Your wing;
What relief to leave our burden,
    Where, for joy, our souls can sing.
This our heaven of contentment,
    Care's distress aside to fling;
Oh the peace of full submission,
    In the presence of our King.

Oh, what wealth we have in heaven,
    Where You sit at God's right hand;
Unto You all power is given,
    Legions wait at Your command.
All is Yours, Oh Christ our Captain,
    All is ours, for while we stand;
On Your promise, faithful Father,
    Taking all Your love has planned.

Priceless promise, powerful Saviour,
    What a hope we have in store;
Hope's dimension but so certain,
    Hope that shineth more and more.
Multitudes that none can number,
    Gathered by the crystal sea;
Could it be, Oh great Redeemer,
    You have prepared a place for me.

At Your Father's throne in heaven,
    There You stand our cause to plead;
God's own Lamb, Who once was wounded,
    Wounds wherein we see our need...
As You raise Your hands, Lord Jesus,
    Graven there, that name my own;
Thus may I, through Jesus only,
    Stand before my Father's throne.

Jesus Christ, our Intercessor,
    Living Lord, for us You pray;;
Praying for Your own, no failure,
    Will O'ertake our souls today.
Then to understand, Oh Master,

    Holy form, bowed low in prayer;
You are at the throne of mercy,
    May love find us ever there.

A Caring Christian

My friend, some words I want to share,
    To let you know that others care;
If only I could take your hand,
    And say, that Christ will understand:
When agony has done its worst,
    It helps to know that on Him first:
The sorrow that your heart has broken,
    Broke His heart, too, but He has spoken;
With open arms He stood and cried,
    "Come unto Me", then at His side;
Find love, and grace and peace divine:
    My friend, look up, the sun will shine.

Sufficient Grace

Oh God, my times are in Your hand,
    My prayer, I want a heart at rest,
How good to know that You have planned,
    Sufficient grace for every test,
I ask for help to understand,
    There is a pillow on Your breast.

Fear Not

Fear not, My child, but take My hand,
    For I have called you by your name;
Be certain that I understand,
    And that My promise you may claim:
Only at My express command,
    Can you be touched by flood or flame;
Trust, every trial can withstand,
    My child, My grace, is just the same.

Just Until the Day Break

My dear one, as you-pass,
    Through the travails of the way,
Oh, remember that God's arm,
    Is round you all the day:
Forget not, there's a heart,
    A safe place where you may stay,
Through Jesus, day will break,
    And all shadows flee away.

Learning To Lean

Dear Lord, my hours, so fast their rate,
So easily it is too late,
Could I but lean on heaven's gate,
And learn, upon the Lord, to wait.

Oh! Those Shoulders

    No shoulder can compare,
        My Shepherd-Friend, to Thine,
    No words or path of prayer,
        Can perfectly define,
    The agony of soul and mind,
        To Him Whose heart is wholly kind,
    My tired, bewildered soul,
        Desires, Oh loving God, in pain,
    Dear Saviour, make me whole,
        And touch me in Your healing name.

Sovereign Storms Over

    Every billow, Lord, I feel,
        Is tempered from above,
    Nor height, nor depth shall ever steal,
        My soul from sovereign love,
    Help me, Oh Master of the waves,
        To cling without a fear,
    And sail with faith and hope toward heaven,
        And know my home is there.

The Cross - His and Mine

There is a cross which I must bear,
 There is a burden I must share,
But I should be without a care,
 Because the Man of Sorrows there,
On that blest cross, His form so fair,
 Was laid on Him my dark despair,
That I might breathe that fragrant air
 And singing go, without a care.

A Time to be Glad

If but for a moment
 I could share a part,
And be glad, for your news
 has so touched my heart;
How lovely to know,
 that away up in heaven
Is One Who is touched
 by the blessing just given.

In Appreciation

"Thank You!" two words
 sincerely meant,
For all the kindness
 you have lent,

Wounds are still wounds
    but healing stands,
To share its love
    with open hands.

My Note to You Today

If my note today should find you,
    In the shadows or in need:
May you understand the grace of God,
    A tower of strength indeed.
By green pastures, by still waters,
    May the kindly Shepherd lead:
Remember that God answers prayer,
    When in Jesus' name we plead.

Thank You

"Inasmuch as you have done it,
You have done it unto Me",
Said the fountainhead of kindness,
Full of love and grace was He,
"But the kindness you have shown me,
And love's token you have given,
Are stored in my heart for ever,
As well as written down in heaven".

Just Being Honest, Lord

Pain comes, but in the mercy of our God,
    Pain passes by;
The haste of life, the stroke of love, and then,
    Aside to lie.
Why this, my Lord, and then what point in pain?
    Why, Lord, to me?
You have seen those weary months, taking toll,
    Lord, did You see?
Oh Christ, Oh do You really understand,
    Just what I say?
Lord, could You, would You just explain to me,
    The 'why' today?
Forgive me, Lord, for coming e'en this way,
    But, Lord, I feel,
I feel unworthy of the call to serve,
    Lord, You can heal,
Lord, the open wound of loneliness.
    No one seems there,
Ah, yes, sometimes I ask concerning You,
    "Where Him, Oh where?"
So hard and cold and unresponsive now,
    Or so it seems.
No one to share those things called visions, Lord,
    Or even dreams,
The heart does ache, thus asking, "Will it break?
    Break with despair?"
Ah, Lord, my heart it feels so cold and hard,
    That even prayer,
Gets crowded out by doing bits of things,

And dashing there,
And rushing here as though just beating air,
Then many a tear,
And always trying to please, Lord, who will hear?
Just being honest, Lord.

The Encourager's Pen

The reason I am writing,
I thought of you today,
I felt I should encourage you,
Along the pilgrim way,
May the sunshine of God's love,
With its strong and gentle ray,
Be the presence of your life,
And may it never pass away.

Amazing Love

Dear Lord, just to know You, in the midst of my days;
Mere words cannot express, what my longing heart prays,
That Your Spirit would lead me in Your blessed ways,
Then my life will be lived to Your glory and praise.

Lord, the only direction my will wants to take;
In Your love and Your mercy, please allow no mistake:
May Your footprints be plain, Lord, as forward I make,
My way to Yourself, 'til that morning shall break.

This poor sinner's heart will be at one with its Lord;
When my love's great ambition receives its reward:
Oh, take all my affections, pray spare not the sword,
'Til my life glorifies You in deed and in word.

Oh that love, Oh to know it, infinitely long,
It bridged the vast gulf between, His right and my wrong:
When my dear Shepherd found me, His shoulder was strong;
Oh that love, Oh my heaven, My Saviour, my song.

Oh that love, to embrace it, so massive and wide,
Like an ocean of mercy, a vast rolling tide:
The love that embraces and yet longs to abide,
In the heart of a life which in love's wounds would hide.

Oh, that love's strong foundation, unfathomed and deep,
Undergirding my life, always able to keep:
When life's shattering storms O'er my soul surely sweep;
My God will not slumber; My Lord will not sleep.

Oh that love, heart aspiring, God's love is so high;
Can you comprehend heaven or understand why?
Christ is far above all but His presence is nigh,
To those who serve urgently while watching the sky.

Oh, love's vast dimension, how I long to explore
Your love satisfies me but I still long for more
Oh, take my capacity and into it pour
That one day in Your Kingdom, I might kneel and adore.

When I Can't Understand

Dear Lord Jesus, there are times,
    When I cannot understand,
Please help me in those moments,
    To stretch out to You my hand,
With love's own reassurance,
    Will You stand right by my side,
Then give me grace to trust You,
    And to lean upon my Guide,
In all of life's dark moments,
    'Till I rise to greet the day,
Then in eternal sunshine,
    Every shadow flees away,
I ask for grace to trust You,
    And to know that through Your word
Will come each timeless promise,
    Just for me, and from the Lord.

Alphabetical List

111	A Beautiful Life
83	Abiding Security
65	A Birthday Prayer
46	About Psalm 33:1-6
112	About Signposts
44	About the 23rd Psalm
116	About the Lord
90	About the Suffering of Jesus
127	A Caring Christian
32	A Close Walk
117	A Home Christ Loved
93	A Living Lord Jesus
133	Amazing Love
101	A More Excellent Way
33	An Aspiring Christian
103	An Open Heart
71	A Praying Christian
111	A Royal Rest
32	A Safe Hiding Place
123	A Sharing Christian
25	Ashes, Agony or Aspiration
130	A Time to be Glad
66	A True Heart Cry
81	Birthdays are Milestones
72	By Prayer and Supplication
28	Changing and Abiding
35	Climb Every Mountain
37	Come Follow Me
109	Cords and the Cross
125	Everything in His Hands
128	Fear Not
107	For a Daughter and Her Mum
104	For the Conversion of St Paul
48	Four Philippian 'Alls'
114	God is Love
87	God's Passover Lamb
104	Grace Did Much More Abound
114	Helping and Caring
53	His Strength Made Perfect
68	I Can't But You Can
130	In Appreciation

84	Infant Wonderful
132	Just Being Honest, Lord
128	Just Until the Day Break
37	Koinonia - Fellowship: Me and the Lord
128	Learning To Lean
51	Let Not Your Heart be Troubled
52	Let This Mind be in You
40	Let Us Go Over
118	Light of the World
35	Lord, I'm Coming Home
123	Lord Jesus, What are You Doing?
34	Lord of My Everything
59	Lord Teach Us How To Pray
30	Make Yourself at Home Lord
36	Making the Most of My Moments
50	Marah - Bitterness
82	Memories of Mother
84	Monarch of the Manger
69	Morning Prayer
92	My Child, Behold My Hands
74	My Morning Dew
131	My Note to You Today
81	New Year Aspirations
85	Oh Bethlehem
75	Oh My Father
129	Oh! Those Shoulders
73	Oh, To Touch You
76	Open! On the Godward Side
72	Prayer Leaps the Barrier of Miles
89	Preciousness Poured Out
54	Pressing Towards the Mark
47	Psalm 121 : A Paraphrase
19	Quest of My life
108	Sea - The Soul Mender
108	Simplicity
119	Sir, the Well is Deep
129	Sovereign Storms Over
127	Sufficient Grace
29	Sunrise - the Break of Day
131	Thank You
23	The Best of My Life
130	The Cross - His and Mine

85	*The Day Star*
76	*The Early Morning Dew*
133	*The Encourager's Pen*
108	*The Eye that Guides*
110	*The Harbour*
105	*The Lane of Life*
90	*The Lord Turned and Looked*
24	*The Love of My Life*
43	*The Love Slave*
121	*The Master's Men*
106	*The Secret of the Shadows*
120	*To Look and Look at Him*
70	*Waiting To Worship*
71	*What are You Saying, Lord?*
67	*What are You Trying to Say, Lord?*
135	*When I Can't Understand*